Foraging for Wild Food in England Summer Edition

OTHER BOOKS FROM GAVIN IRELAND AND FOUND FOOD

MY FORAGING JOURNAL

This small notebook is perfect for foragers to record their finds, making sure that they can find them again in the future, and also to learn from experiences about environmental influences on places where specific plants/mushrooms are likely to grow.

THE FORAGER'S GUIDE TO BOTANY

As your interest, knowledge and skills develop as a forager, you'll notice unfamiliar, sometimes seemingly impenetrable language used by "experts". You could be forgiven for thinking that you need to study for a botany degree to understand it all, but no more.

After reading The Forager's Guide to Botany you'll have a good understanding of the botanical terminology and concepts needed to advance your foraging learning.

FORAGING FOR WILD FOOD IN ENGLAND – SPRING EDITION

A handy small book highlighting common springtime plants to be found in England, and some general introductory information about foraging.

FORAGING FOR WILD FOOD IN ENGLAND – AUTUMN EDITION

A handy small book highlighting common autumn plants to be found in England, and some general introductory information about foraging.

FORAGING FOR WILD FOOD IN ENGLAND COOKBOOK

A handy small companion to the Foraging for Wild Food in England series, with handy recipes for the common edible plants and fungi found in that series.

ALSO AVAILABLE THROUGH FOUNDFOOD.COM

Since 2010, Found Food has been helping foraging enthusiasts to learn more about their surroundings and how they can best make use of the natural resources all around.

THE FORAGER HELPER

The Forager Helper is a repository of the knowledge that Gavin has built up over the years or foraging, wildcrafting, and studying. At the time of publishing there were over 100 plant, tree, and fungi monographs, videos, recipes, and plant and fungi family descriptions.

Find out more at www.foragerhelper.foundfood.com

SIMPLE BOTANY FOR FORAGERS

This is an online course which this book was designed to accompany. It includes video chapters, quizzes, and downloadable information sheets.

FACE-TO-FACE FORAGING WALKS

You can book face-to-face foraging walks covering Introductions to Foraging, Forage and Feast (which includes a foraging themed picnic), and Forage and Cook (which includes cooking a meal using the things we've foraged along the way), or you can request a custom walk/course.

FORAGING COACHING

If you're looking to become a foraging teacher, or just want to develop your skills and deepen your understanding, a series of coaching calls can help you to achieve that.

Copyright ©2024 Found Food Ltd

All photos by Gavin Ireland.

All rights reserved. No part of this book may be reproduced by any mechanical, photographic, or electronic process, or in the form of a phonographic recording; nor may it be stored in a retrieval system, transmitted, or otherwise copied for public or private use – other than for "fair use" as brief quotations embedded in articles and reviews – without prior written permission of the publisher and FoundFood.com.

The author of this book does not dispense medical advice or prescribe the use of any technique as a form of treatment for physical, emotional, or medical problems without the advice of a physician, either directly or indirectly. The intent of the author is only to provide information of a general nature to help you to learn more about botany, plant identification and usage of those plants. In the event that you use any of the information in this book for yourself or others, the author and publisher assume no responsibility for your actions.

Table of Contents

Introduction 8
    Foraging in England 8
    So why do you want to go foraging? 9

Part 1 - Building the Foundations of Foraging 10
    The power of wild food for nutrition and medicine 10
    Getting to know where you live 12
        Choose a spot to get to know really well 13
        Your foraging journal 14
    Foraging principles 16
        The law 16
        Your responsibility 17
        Awareness of harvesting 18
    Poisonous plants to watch out for 19
    Poison Hemlock (*Conium maculatum*). 20
    Hemlock Water Dropwort (*Oenanthe crocata*). 21
    Foxglove (Digitalis purpurea) 22
    Lords and Ladies (*Arum maculatum*) 23
    Giant Hogweed (Heracleum mantegazzianum) 24
    Dog's Mercury (Mercurialis perennis) 25

Part 2 - Summer Foraging 26
    Blackberries (*Rubus fruticosus*) 28
    Elderflower (*Sambucus nigra*) 34
    Common Mallow (*Malva sylvestris*) 40
    Mugwort (*Artemisia vulgaris*) 44
    Silverweed (*Argentina anserina*) 50
    Yarrow (*Achillea millefolium*) 54

Wild Strawberries (*Fragaria vesca*) 60
Wild Rose Petals (*Rosa canina*) 64
Elderberry (*Sambucus nigra*) 70
Bilberry (*Vaccinium myrtillus*) 76
Penny Bun (*Boletus edulis*) 80

Next Steps **83**
About The Author **84**

INTRODUCTION

FORAGING IN ENGLAND

England is full of unique and beautiful environments, which sit alongside cultural attractions and its amazing cities and countryside. With rivers, lakes and canals, the many and varied national parks, and areas of outstanding natural beauty, and a wide variety of wild plants, fungi, and animals.

English countryside

England is the centre of the United Kingdom with a temperate climate and environments as diverse as rain forests, cities and towns, craggy windswept highlands, and warm, sheltered lowlands. The clear seas, bright harbours and hidden coves of the coastline give way to busy market towns and the tranquillity of lush green valleys, rolling hills, and shimmering lakes.

As the early growth of spring leads into the heat of summer, England shows off its heavy growth of foliage, flowers, and fruit,, inviting visitors to experience the beauty and excitement of the region. From the rolling hills to the tranquil shores, nature adorns the landscape with blackberries, strawberries, and porcini, creating an edible landscape straight out of a storybook.

A lot of the edible and medicinal plants and fungi of the UK can be found in many places, what tends to vary is how common and widespread they are, so this guide focusses on the plants and fungi that are common and widespread in England. For example, Porcini mushrooms (*Boletus edulis*) can be found in many places the UK, but it is very common in England.

So why do you want to go foraging?

It could be that you're looking at the survival aspect and you want to know that you could survive on wild food if you needed to; it could be that you're looking to reduce your carbon footprint and packaging waste by using more local ingredients in your diet; or maybe you're looking to reduce your food bill by using free ingredients from nature; or you want to introduce some new flavours into your diet which you would otherwise never experience. Maybe for you it's a combination of two or more of those reasons, it doesn't really matter because the principles remain the same. Whatever your reasons it's important to know how to go about it safely, responsibly, and legally.

Part 1 - Building the Foundations of Foraging

The power of wild food for nutrition and medicine

The human "diet" was once seasonal, and highly varied. Given that different food plants have a wide spectrum of micro-nutrients, and that our modern diet consists of much less variety, how much nutrition and culinary medicine are we missing out on?

As far back as records go, there is evidence that we used plants for medicine, and regardless of what type of diet you follow and why, our physiology tells us that we are designed to be omnivorous (meaning our bodies are equipped to deal with meat and plants in our diet), therefore it is a safe assumption that we get a large proportion of our nutrition from the plants that we eat. Indeed, it is possible and is evidenced every day that humans can thrive on a diet of plant-based food alone, whilst the same cannot be said of a solely meat-based diet. Over thousands of years, the human race has developed increasingly efficient methods to produce vast quantities of food crops for consumption, and at the same time we've learned how to make the crops uniform, brightly coloured and sweeter to appeal to modern human cravings. Sometimes all of this advancement has been at the cost of nutrition and goodness.

Of the estimated 400,000 plant species on the planet, approximately 300,000 could be eaten, yet human beings eat around 200 species and of those, 3 species contribute to our plant-sourced protein and calories: maize, rice, and wheat. Given that our habit of eating only a few plant species is a relatively new thing, over the last 200 years or so, how much nutrition and medicine are we missing out on? One might even draw connections between this and the increase in cancers, arthritis, and other life-limiting illnesses over a similar period. That's a bigger question than can be answered in a foraging book but suffice to say that I've never felt better since foraging regularly and I hear the same thing from other foragers too.

This book does not cover the subject of herbalism, that would need a series of books to itself! However, where appropriate I will mention of few of the medicinal properties of the plants we look at in the following sections. Most of our modern medicines are extracts of or synthesised from plants or fungus, so foraging for medicinal plants is also a practice experiencing a revival too.

Getting to know where you live

If we're all so concerned nowadays about reducing our carbon footprints and trying to reverse the environmental damage we cause, why are so many people totally unaware of the food that grows all around them? We can all do our bit by trying to avoid buying produce that has travels hundreds of miles or using public/human powered transport to get to the shops, but we can also look at what's growing right outside our door.

Where you live will have a profound effect on which wild plants grow near you, whether they are thriving or merely surviving, their nutritional values and potentially whether they are safe to consume or not.

From a geographical point of view England is in a temperate climate zone, meaning that we do not experience the extremes of temperatures which you might see in the equatorial or polar zones. However, in England we also have a very wet environment with relatively high levels of rainfall Also, within our temperate zone you'll find differences depending on whether you live in a city, a forest, an agricultural area, on the coast and so on. This small book cannot cover all of those environments, so it is up to you to use some basic principles and really get to know where you live.

The first step is to really observe. Not just make a note that you live in a suburban area of a temperate region. What grows really well where you are? Does a particular type of tree seem to pop up everywhere? Does one type of weed appear in every pavement crack? Does it seem that no matter how much you search you can never find that plant which seems common and widespread everywhere else? This first step of getting to know where you live also becomes your first step to learning about more plants. At the early stages, instead of spending time learning about an interesting plant and searching in vain, choose the plants you see all the time, learn what they are, understand their lifecycle and see if they can be of any use to you.

CHOOSE A SPOT TO GET TO KNOW REALLY WELL

One of the best ways I've found to get to know and to connect with my local area, is to find a safe, accessible spot where I can sit and observe. Sometimes it's only for ten minutes, sometimes for hours, but the key is that it needs to be somewhere that I can keep going back to throughout the year. Your spot can be under a tree, on a park bench, or anywhere you choose where you can peacefully observe nature. Your first choice of spot may not turn out to be the best, so be prepared to find another one. If you have the time, maybe you'll have several spots, but remember you're here to observe and learn as well as to relax and enjoy being outside.

This is where your journal can come in handy, noting what grows and when, describing the weather, how you're feeling, volume of other people and animals and so on. It can also be the place to make a note of whether you'll return there or not, and if not, why?

YOUR FORAGING JOURNAL

First and foremost, my journal acts as an aide-memoire for all of the wonderful things I've seen and would like to be able to find again one day. I've lost track of the number of times over the years I've found myself in the correct season for Porcini mushrooms, for example, but I can't remember where I saw them! Was it local, or while I was away somewhere? If it was local, where exactly was it? Once I started journaling, it saved me a lot of time finding plants, trees, and mushrooms.

Things to consider for your journal:

- Describe where you are and how to get there.
- The closest large geographical feature (e.g., coastline, mountains, forests, lakes etc.)
- What is the soil like? (e.g., sticky, crumbly, thin, etc.)
- What are the levels of rainfall like? How hot and cold does it get?
- List some common trees you can identify – if you don't know their names yet, describe/draw/photograph them.
- List some common plants you can identify – if you don't know their names yet, describe/draw/photograph them.
- List some common fungi you can identify – if you don't know their names yet, describe/draw/photograph them.
- List some common insects you can identify, and the plants you see them on or around – if you don't know their names yet, describe/draw/photograph them.
- List some common animals you can identify, and the plants you see them on or around – if you don't know their names yet, describe/draw/photograph them.
- List some common birds you can identify, and the plants you see them on or around – if you don't know their names yet, describe/draw/photograph them.

- Consider whether the plants and animals you've identified are native, introduced, invasive or even endangered.
- Are there native/first people in the area? Who are they?
- Is there a local history of plant/land usage?
- Where does drinking water come from and where does waste water go?
- Who are your neighbours here?

These can be quite difficult questions to answer sometimes, so consider approaching local people that have been around a long time, local historians, local teachers, gardening and allotment groups, field guides, libraries and museums, park groups/societies, environmental organisations, and local universities/colleges.

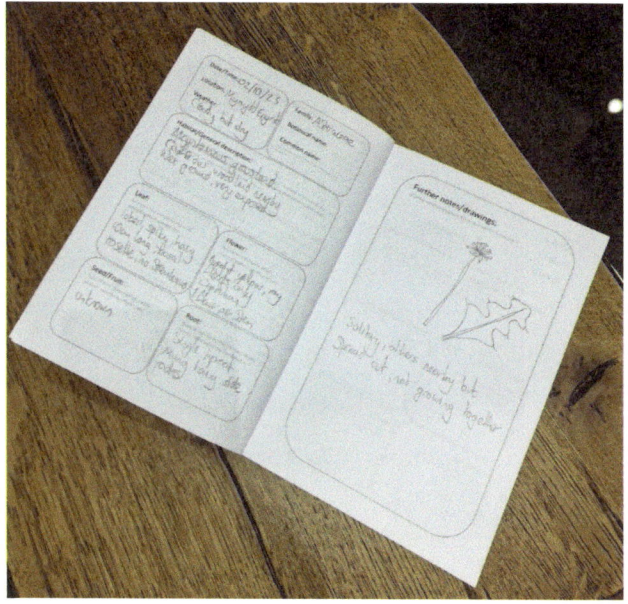

You can find a downloadable, printable version of my template here: https://foundfood.com/wp-content/uploads/2024/01/Journal_download.pdf

Or buy a pre-printed book of journal pages here: https://shop.foundfood.com/products/my-foraging-journal

Foraging principles

Our principles are the high-level rules by which we live our lives. They are self-imposed, not dictated to us, a moral code if you will. We can break other people's rules and still feel OK about ourselves (in some situations), but when we go against our own principles it usually feels pretty bad.

What are foraging principles? Well, to me principles are high-level beliefs and considerations, foraging morals maybe, general non-specific guidelines that you can take with you wherever you are in the world and on your foraging journey.

Blackberry bush

THE LAW

The first thing we need to be mindful of is the law. The overriding principle is this: "Be aware and respectful of the laws and rules relating to foraging where you are." Not knowing what the laws are is not an acceptable excuse to police or to courts.

Within the UK, there are different rules and laws depending on where you are. In England, if you have the right to be there then you can be confident that it's OK foraging leaves, flowers, fruits, seeds, fungus, and bark (responsibly and carefully harvested); However, if you want to collect roots, or do anything else that may cause serious or lasting harm, you need to have the landowner's permission. Contrary to popular belief, just about all land in England is owned by someone, even "common land". You should also be aware of any "protected species" – certain plants are listed as protected because they are endangered, and we don't want them to disappear altogether. Generally, you won't be likely to forage any of those plants, but it is important to be aware of them. Finally, in England we also have bylaws, which are locally enacted laws which may apply restrictions to foraging activity. Now, you'll find lots of advice about the legality of certain rules and regulations on the internet, and from certain experts, but if you ever end up in court. the buck stops with you; so, make sure you're aware of the rules and understand the risks.

YOUR RESPONSIBILITY

As a forager, I take on the responsibility for caring for the environment that I take from. It's not as simple as "only taking what you need", although that's very important. It's not just about "do no harm", which again is important too.

Trampled wild garlic (Allium ursinum)

When I see a patch of wild garlic that has been trampled to mud, stripped of any sign of the plants, and surrounding plants damaged,

I'm not only saddened, disgusted and angry, I'm also thinking how can I fix this? Yes, it's not my fault, and yes I might be fixing it only to have the same thing happen again, but maybe someone will see the cared for and nurtured spot and think twice about doing it again, maybe I can reduce the knock-on damage to the surrounding habitat and make it better for the future.

Likewise, when I see piles of litter in my environment, yes, it's not my fault, yes it's not my job to pick it up, but if everyone thinks like that, the litter will harm the plants and wildlife in my environment and I don't want that.

AWARENESS OF HARVESTING

There are many self-imposed rules out there that foragers will use and share, such as only pick from every tenth plant, or only take 40% of what's available; but I would suggest that a little more care is needed. For example, consider how abundant the plant is locally – some plants are plentiful in some parts and scarce in others, if the plant is scarce where you are maybe consider not taking any at all. Which stage of the growth cycle is the plant in? Would harvesting it now prevent its continued growth cycle? How healthy are these particular plants? Maybe you can help to nurture this area so you can harvest in the future when it's better?

Poisonous plants to watch out for

The majority of plants are safe to handle, and a lot are safe to consume, however there are some that can cause discomfort, sickness and even death. The worst of these are the ones that look a lot like good edible plants. So, as well as learning plant families for identification, it's also worth learning the common dangerous species in isolation too. Here are six common and widespread dangerous plants in England worth knowing:

POISON HEMLOCK (*CONIUM MACULATUM*).

Poison hemlock leaves

From the *Apiaceae* family we mentioned earlier, eating Hemlock usually results in death. It can grow as tall as 15 feet, with a hollow stem that usually has purple splotches on it. One of the things that makes it so dangerous is that it looks just like some kind of wild parsley, especially around the leaves and flowers. It can be difficult to tell the difference between this and cow parsley (*Anthriscus sylvestris*).

HEMLOCK WATER DROPWORT (*OENANTHE CROCATA*).

Hemlock water dropwort leaves

This is another member of the *Apiaceae* family. Again, highly poisonous, usually causing death; and again, so dangerous because the above ground parts look like celery, and the roots look a lot like water parsnip (all also *Apiaceae*).

FOXGLOVE (DIGITALIS PURPUREA)

Foxglove flowers

Foxglove can cause severe sickness and death if you eat it. The toxins in Digitalis can act pretty quickly on the heart and stop it from working. Very common in and near woodland, and very pretty, it has a basal rosette of velvety soft-haired leaves and a tall spike of bell-shaped flowers (usually purple or pink). Sometimes the young leaves are confused with Comfrey and Mullein.

LORDS AND LADIES (*ARUM MACULATUM*)

Arum flower and leaves

This plant has many, many common names so demonstrating the importance of scientific names! Unlike the previous plants, Arum is not strictly speaking poisonous; However, it has microscopic, needle-sharp crystals that can pierce the cell walls of your mucous membranes. For most people that have experienced this, it means the most intense and painful pins and needles in your lips tongue and mouth, along with inflammation and swelling, all of which lasts at least a few hours. That alone is bad enough, but imagine you swallowed it instead of spitting it out? The same reaction in your throat causes swelling that you are unable to breathe and therefore causes death.

Giant Hogweed (Heracleum mantegazzianum).

Giant hogweed leaves

Back to the *Apiaceae* family again, I did say it had lots of dangerous species! Giant hogweed sap can cause photodermatitis, which when exposed to sunlight causes extreme sunburn and blistering. Some people have reported symptoms from merely touching the leaves or stem; However, in most cases, it is from cutting or breaking the plant and coming into contact with the sap. It can't be simply washed off (although you should remove it from your skin to prevent further damage) and can remain active for many years. It's related namesake, Common Hogweed (*Heracleum sphondylium*) is a common and popular edible and can look similar when young. Giant hogweed grows to 20 feet tall, with wide spreading umbels of white flowers. It has thick ridged stems with purple splotches, and unlike common hogweed has shiny, hairless leaves.

Dog's Mercury (Mercurialis perennis)

Dog's mercury leaves and flowers

This can cause vomiting, jaundice, coma, and death from eating it. It is a very common woodland plant, and although it doesn't look much like edible plants, it is so common and widespread that it would be easy to accidentally grab a few stems whilst harvesting wild garlic, nettles, ground ivy etc.

Looking at plant families can seem overwhelming, now I've added a small handful of the toxic plants to look out for too! Sorry about that, but it's important to at least be aware of them until you can confidently identify them. Also, it is a lot to learn, but what can help is to pick a common local plant and get to know it well, before moving onto the next, rather than trying to learn about them all and getting stuck.

Part 2 - Summer Foraging

I'm often asked, "which is the best month for foraging?", or "Which is the best season?" and frustratingly my answer is usually something along the lines of "they're all great, it just depends on what you're looking for".

Summer has the advantage of longer, warmer days and evenings for foraging which makes the whole experience a little nicer. Summer also has the sweetness of berries and other fruit starting to appear, whilst still holding onto the delicate green herbs of spring.

Summer means fruit, flowers and leaves for eating and for cooking, herbs still coming through for flavouring, and late summer mushrooms such as porcini (also known as cepe, or penny bun) make themselves available.

Remembering that this is supposed to be a getting started guide, I've selected some common, easy to recognise and easy to use summer plants to get you started. Each plant includes as much information as I thought you might need (or could stand at this early stage).

BLACKBERRIES (*RUBUS FRUTICOSUS*)

In other parts of the world, bramble is used to mean any prickly shrub. Here in the UK we use it to mean the blackberry bush, *Rubus fruticosus*. That isn't where the complication ends though, *Rubus fruticosus* (or *Rubus fruticosus* agg.) is in fact a grouping of over 375 closely related microspecies of plants! The good news is that they're all edible and we can treat them all in the same way.

KEY INFORMATION

Common names: Bramble, blackberry bush, shrubby blackberry.

Botanical name: *Rubus fruticosus*

Family: *Roseacea*

Parts used: Flowers, fruit, stems, and leaves.

DISTRIBUTION

Rubus Fruticosus is mostly limited to Western Europe and Western Scandanavia, however the closely related blackberry species are to be found across Europe, north-western Africa, western and central Asia and north and south America.

HABITAT

There aren't many habitats that Bramble doesn't like. Hedgerows, woodland, meadows, especially common on waste ground.

HOW TO IDENTIFY BRAMBLE

Bramble is a fast growing and spreading deciduous shrub, growing up to 3m by 3m and spreading quickly to overtake wasteland, scrub and un-tended gardens. It can grow taller if supported by other plants, or its own bushiness, and can grow much longer when trailing along the ground.

The stem has a woody core and can grow up to 2cm thick. Usually covered in sharp, curved prickles. Sometimes the stem has a star-shaped cross section. In the first year the stem grows quickly producing many leaves but no flowers. In the second year the main stem doesn't grow any longer but it produces flowering side stems.

The leaves are large, green, palmately compound with five or seven leaflets. The flowering stems' leaves are smaller, with three or five leaflets.

The flowers are produced in late spring and early summer on short racemes on the tips of the flowering stems. Each flower is about 2–3 cm in diameter, with five white or pale pink petals. Bramble does not flower in the first year.

The fruit, or drupelets grow in bunches around a central "core" and together they form an aggregate fruit, or what we call the blackberry. They appear and ripen to nearly black in the autumn after pollination.

Ripe blackberry fruit

Food

The fruit Can be eaten raw or cooked and there can't be many people that haven't tried it. They fruit can range from sour and strong flavoured to sweet and subtly flavoured depending on variety and how ripe they are. The fruit is also made into syrups, jams, and other preserves, and wine.

The leaves are one of my favourite walking/foraging snacks. When the leaf buds are just opened, but the leaves are not yet spread out, pick off a small bunch and eat. You need to chew them at the back of your mouth until your mouth juices start flowing (they are quite drying at first), then you get the most amazing, complex, savoury flavour comes through. The opened, but still young leaves can be made into a refreshing tea, and the dried leaves are often used in herbal tea blends.

The root can be eaten cooked, but it needs a lot of boiling. Not something I've been tempted to try yet.

The very young shoots can be harvested early in the spring as they emerge from the ground, peeled and eaten raw in salads. You can also wait until they're 5-8mm in diameter, slice into 2-3mm slices and pickle or candy the shoots to make nice star-shaped snacks (some stems have a star-shaped cross section).

Medicine

A decoction of the leaves can be used as a gargle to treat sore throats, mouth ulcers, gum inflammation and also makes a good general mouthwash. Large quantities of the leaves can have a laxative effect.

Known hazards

Apart from the nasty prickles, none known but some people have has stomach upset from eating too many sour (under-ripe) berries.

Harvesting

The leaves are usually out from early spring and you can find those tasty leaf buds most of the year if you look hard enough. The fruit can be picked from August to October.

Bramble leaves

POTENTIAL LOOKALIKES

As mentioned above, there are hundreds of micro species of *R. fruticosus* so you may find a little variation in looks, but they are all edible.

MYTHOLOGY AND SYMBOLISM

In the UK it's traditional not to pick blackberries after Old Michaelmas day (11 October) as the Devil will have fouled on them. In Ireland a similar story tells of the Pooka urinating on the berries at Halloween. Generally the fruit is past its best then anyway.

According to some stories, the dark purple colour of the fruit juice represents Christ's blood from the crown of bramble thorns he was made to wear. However, there are just as many stories claiming the thorns to have been other plants such as hawthorn or euphorbia.

Other superstition about bramble includes that stains from the fruit won't come out of clothes with the fruiting season is still on; hair is more likely to fall out during blackberry season, if a girl's dress gets caught by bramble prickles whilst walking with her boyfriend, he will be faithful; and a good blackberry season means a good herring season. In Christian tradition, the 5 ribs of the leaf represent the 5 wounds that Christ received at his crucifixion.

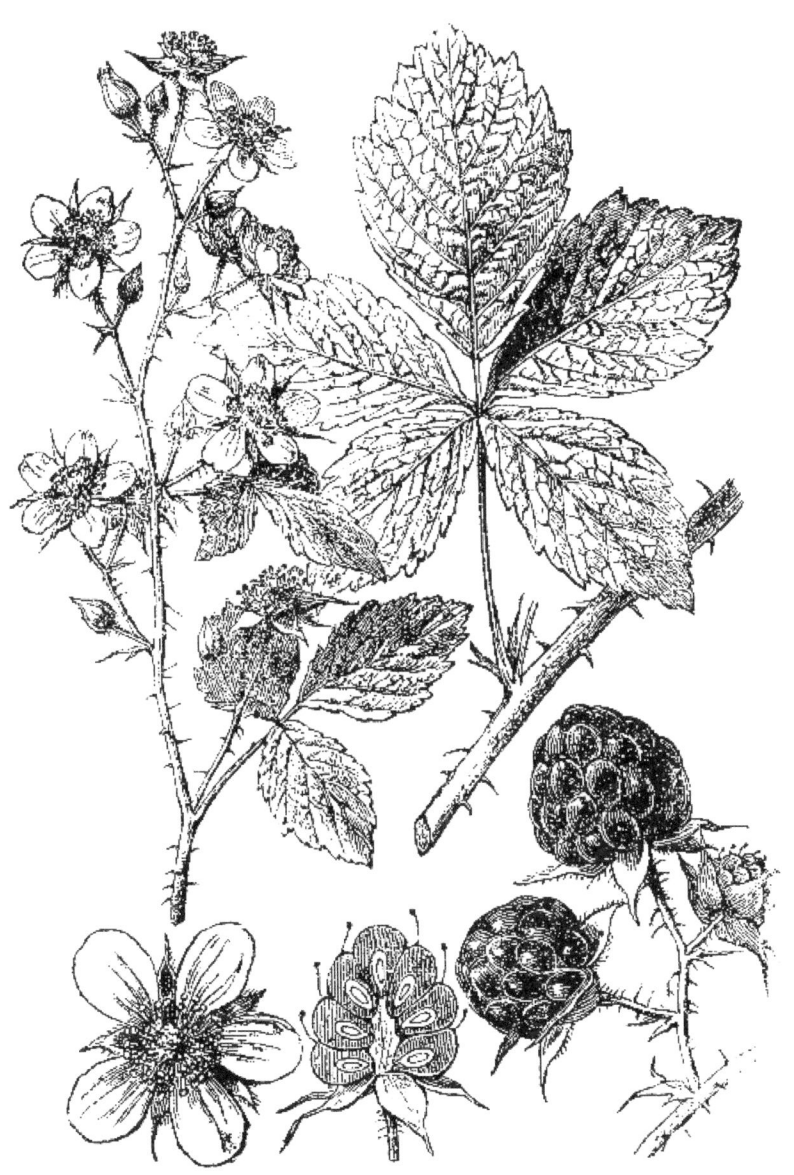

ELDERFLOWER (*SAMBUCUS NIGRA*)

According to tradition, if you want to take from the Elder tree you must ask the tree's permission. If the tree makes any sound at all, the answer is no; To take from the tree without permission means a curse and certain bad luck until you make amends...

KEY INFORMATION

Common names: Elder, elderberry, European black elderberry, European elder, European elderberry.

Botanical name: *Sambucus nigra*

Family: *Adoxaceae*

Parts used: flowers, and fruit.

Distribution

It is widespread in many temperate and sub-tropical regions of the world, and is native to the UK.

Habitat

Elder will grow in both wet and dry fertile soils, but in very wet soil the growth and fruiting can be heavily stunted. Primarily in sunny locations in woodland, scrub, hedgerows and wasteland. It often grows near rabbit warrens and badger setts where the seeds are distributed by animal droppings.

How to identify elder

Elder is usually found as a shrub or small tree (usually up to 6 meters, but has been recorded up to 10 meters) and can live for 60 years. It is commonly characterised by its short trunk.

Like many other small trees it can grow as an upright tree or a straggly bush depending on the conditions and how it is cut back.

The bark is grey-brown, corky, deeply furrowed bark, although younger specimens have smooth grey bark.

The green unpleasant smelling twigs are hollow or have a white pith (spongy tissue) inside. New stems sometimes grow directly upwards when a branch has been cut or broken.

Buds have a ragged appearance often with leaves showing through the bud scales.

The leaves are pinnate with two to three opposite pairs (rarely four pairs) and a terminal leaflet. The leaflets are oval shaped and toothed and tend to be five to twelve centimetres long. The leaves can make an unpleasant smell when crushed.

Borne on large flat umbels, 10-30cm across, the individual flowers are tiny, creamy coloured, highly scented, and have five petals and five stamen. The smell is often compared to cat pee, but I find it quite pleasant.

Elders are hermaphrodite, meaning both the male and female reproductive parts are contained within the same flower. After pollination by insects, each flower develops into a small, purple-black, sour berry, which ripens from late-summer to autumn.

Food

The flowers can be used raw or cooked. They can also be dried for later use. The flowers are crisp and somewhat juicy, they have an aromatic smell and flavour and are delicious raw as a refreshing snack on a summers day, though look out for the insects. The flowers are used to add a muscatel flavour to stewed fruits, jellies and jams (especially gooseberry jam). They are often used to make a sparkling wine. A sweet tea is made from the dried flowers.

Some of the flowers can smell a little "off", occasionally compared to cat pee. This can sometimes happen when the flowers are getting older.

Medicine

Elder has a very long history of household use as a medicinal herb and is also much used by herbalists. The plant has been called 'the medicine chest of country people'.

The flowers are the main part used in modern herbalism, though all parts of the plant have been used at times. The flowers, berries, leaves and bark have been used in medicinal preparations including Elderflower water for skin and eye complaints, inner bark for constipation and arthritic conditions, leaves for bruises and sprains, and fruit and flowers for colds and flu.

Known hazards

Every part of this plant, apart from the flowers and ripe berries, are considered toxic and should not be ingested. Some sensitivity to the ripe berries has been reported, and for those people the berries must be cooked before ingestion.

Other varieties of Sambucus have toxic berries, including the red-berried elder (for example).

Harvesting

The flowers appear from late June and can persist into August.

Potential lookalikes

Walnut (*Juglans regia*), however, elder has oppositely arranged leaves whereas walnut has alternately arranged leaves.

Identified in winter by the green unpleasant smelling twigs are hollow or have a white pith (spongy tissue) inside. Buds have a ragged appearance often with leaves showing through the bud scales.

OTHER USES

Elder wood is hard and yellow-white. Mature wood is used for whittling and carving, while smaller stems can be hollowed out to make craft items.

Elder foliage was once used to keep flies away and branches were often hung around dairies. It can also be used as an emergency insect repellent by rubbing the leaves together to get the juice out and smearing it on your skin; Be warned, it will temporarily turn your skin green and also act as a friend repellent as it smells bad.

Elder is also a great source for a variety of coloured dyes and historically it was used to make lushly patterned Harris Tweed. Blue and purple dye was obtained from the berries, yellow and green from the leaves, and grey and black dye was made from the bark.

ELDER AND WILDLIFE

The flowers provide nectar for a variety of insects and the berries are eaten by birds and mammals. Small mammals such as dormice and bank voles eat both the berries and the flowers.

Many moth caterpillars feed on elder foliage, including the white spotted pug, swallowtail, dot moth and buff ermine.

MYTHOLOGY AND SYMBOLISM

There is a lot of mythology, folklore and symbolism surrounding the Elder; Here is a selection of some of the things I've read/heard:

It is thought the name elder comes the Anglo-saxon 'aeld', meaning fire, because the hollow stems were used as bellows to blow air into the centre of a fire.

It was thought that if you burned elder wood you would see the devil, but if you planted elder by your house it would keep the devil away.

Elder was also known as Judas' Tree as it was believed that Judas Iscariot hanged himself on an Elder tree.

In England it was said that if you made a baby's crib from Elder wood, the elder mother would pull the baby's legs and pinch them so they would get no rest. According to an Irish superstition, animals and children would stop growing when beaten with an elder stick.

There are stories of various types of trees which apparently cannot be struck by lightning and Elder is no exception. Apparently Elder cannot be struck by lightning because Christ's cross was made from Elder. Please don't believe this one, there are no trees that cannot be struck!

Common Mallow (*Malva sylvestris*)

This common weed has such brightly coloured flowers that you could be forgiven for thinking that it had escaped from a garden; But no, this is not only one of our native wild plants, but also very useful for food.

Key information

Common names: Cheeses, French hollyhock, high mallow, tall mallow, tree mallow.

Botanical name: *Malva sylvestris*

Family: *Malvaceae*

Parts used: Leaves, flowers, and seeds.

Distribution

Native to western Europe, Malva sylvestris is now naturalised in eastern Australia, USA, Canada and Mexico where it is considered an invasive species. It can be found in the wild all across Europe, northern Africa and the Arabian peninsula and Asia.

Habitat

Woodland sunny spots, hedgerows, meadows, near footpaths, and gardens. Not usually found in acid soils.

How to identify common mallow

A fast growing perennial/biennial which can grow up to 50cm tall unsupported. It has large leaves, bright mauve/purple flowers and seed pods shaped like a cheese wheel, hence the common name "cheeses".

The leaves are round, but divided where the stem joins, and usually with 5 shallow lobes of varying depths. They are usually up to 10cm in diameter although can grow larger, and have hairs radiating from the centre. The leaves sometimes have a purple spot in the middle which, also sometimes extends down the petiole.

The flowers are a pinkish-mauve with dark purple strips. The colour can vary slightly. They grow in axillary clusters of two to four flowers on the stem. Usually the flowers start opening at the bottom of the plant first, rising to the top. The five petals are very narrow at the base, getting wider at the outside where they are slightly notched in the middle.

The fruit or seed pods are nutlets, sometimes called cheeses, and up to 1cm in diameter; Shaped like cheese wheels. They are green to begin with and start to brown as they ripen.

Food

Leaves can be eaten raw or cooked. They are quite thick/mucilaginous and have a pleasant mild flavour. They can be chopped or blitzed into soups where they act as a thickener, roasted to make crisps, or used in place of vine leaves for dolmades. Mallow leaves have been used as a tea substitute.

Flowers can be eaten raw. Added to salads or desserts as a garnish, a pleasant mild flavour.

The seeds, also known as cheese wheels have a nutty flavour when eaten as a nibble.

Medicine

All parts of the plant are antiphlogistic, astringent, demulcent, diuretic, emollient, expectorant, laxative, salve. The leaves and flowers are the main part used, their demulcent properties making them valuable as a poultice for bruise, inflammations, insect bites etc.

Known hazards

None known.

Harvesting

Common mallow starts to appear from late May and will usually persist into October.

The leaves can be gathered any time, although it is good practice to allow the plant to get established first. Because of their demulcent nature, the leaves lose a lot of their usefulness as food if you dry them for later use, however dried they can be used as a tea substitute.

The flowers can be harvested from June and can be dried for later use.

The "cheeses" are usually about from late august onwards.

Potential lookalikes

Other mallows can look similar but are edible.

Geraniums can have similar leaf shapes, but have a distinctive smell, whereas mallow leaves don't have a noticeable smell.

Mythology and symbolism

It was said that planting common mallow on graves would feed the dead.

In Ireland, common mallow was one of the seven herbs that protect against evil spirits, including eyebright, self-heal, speedwell, St. John's wort, vervain, and yarrow.

Mugwort (*Artemisia vulgaris*)

Mugwort was used extensively to flavour and preserve ale before the discovery of hops. I have to say, one of my favourite home brew flavourings so far...

Key information

Common names: Chrysanthemum weed, common wormwood, felon herb, jack bacca, moxa, naughty man, old man, old uncle Henry, riverside wormwood, wild wormwood.

Botanical name: *Artemisia vulgaris*

Family: *Asteraceae*

Parts used: Flowers, and leaves.

Distribution

Throughout most temperate regions of the northern hemisphere, including Britain.

Habitat

Common on hedge banks and waysides, uncultivated and waste land. It likes nitrogenous soils so is commonly found on roadsides and wasteland, and alongside stinging nettles and other "weedy" plants.

How to identify mugwort

Artemisia vulgaris is a tall herbaceous perennial plant growing 1–2 m tall, with a woody root and extensive rhizomes. Whilst it can spread by seed, it also spread by those rhizomes. The leaves are 5–20 cm long, dark green, pinnate and sessile, with dense, short, white, downy hairs on the underside. The stiff stems are grooved and sometimes have a reddish tinge. The small florets (5 mm long) are radially symmetrical with many yellow or red petals. The narrow and numerous capitula (flower heads), all fertile, spread out in racemose panicles. It flowers from mid-summer to early autumn.

FOOD

The leaves can be eaten raw or cooked, they are very aromatic and somewhat bitter. Their addition to the diet aids the digestion and so they are often used in small quantities as a flavouring, especially with fatty foods. They are also used to give colour and flavour to Mochi (glutinous-rice dumplings) in Japan. The young shoots are used in spring. In Japan the young leaves are used as a potherb. The dried leaves and flowering tops are steeped into tea. They have also been used as a flavouring in beer, though fell into virtual disuse once hops came into favour – I can vouch for the fact that Mugwort makes an excellent home brewed beer.

MEDICINE

Mugwort has a long history of use in herbal medicine especially in matters connected to the digestive system, menstrual complaints and the treatment of worms. It is slightly toxic, however, and should never be used by pregnant women, especially in their first trimester, since it can cause a miscarriage.

Mugwort flowers

Known hazards

Being a member of the Asteraceae family, skin contact can cause dermatitis in some people. Probably unsafe for pregnant women as it may stimulate the uterus to contract and induce abortion.

Harvesting

The leaves are harvested in August and can be dried for later use.

The roots are harvested in the autumn and dried for later use in medicinal preparations.

Potential lookalikes

There are many species in the Artemisia genus and some can look superficially similar. Be certain that you have the correct species for using it for anything.

Mythology and symbolism

There is a legend that St. John the Baptist wore a girdle of Mugwort, and garlands made from plants cured in the smoke from St. John's Eve bonfires were believed to protect a home from evil.

Known in the Middle Ages as Mater Herbarum (mother of herbs), Mugwort was held sacred by various cultures and thought to be the oldest of plants. In particular it was believed to be a plant that offered protection to humans. It was once common to hang a sprig of mugwort over the doorway — or to burn it as an incense — to keep illness and evil spirits away from the home.

The 'mug' in Mugwort is said by some to be derived from an old word for 'moth', the plant once having been used (like moth-balls) to protect clothes against hungry moths. The nicer, although less likely belief is that the 'mug' referred to is to do with the vessel that ale was drunk from; In common with a number of other herbs, Mugwort was used to flavour beer in the days before hops were introduced. Its dried leaves have also been used as substitutes for both tea and tobacco (hence the old Norfolk name of 'Jack bacca').

The properties of Mugwort, or muggons, seem to have been well known to Scottish mermaids. This was the advice reputed to have been sung by one such as she watched a young girl's funeral processing along the banks of the Firth of Clyde:-

If they wad drink nettles in March

And eat muggons in May,

Sae mony braw maidens

Wadna gang to the clay.

Mugwort and Wildlife

A number of species of Lepidoptera (butterflies and moths) feed on the leaves and flowers.

Silverweed (*Argentina anserina*)

The yellow flowering plant of the dusty wayside with silvery fern-like leaves that lay flat on the ground has been called the Footsteps of Our Lord.

Key information

Common names: Potentilla anserina, common silverweed, silver cinquefoil, the footsteps of our lord.

Botanical name: *Argentina anserina*

Family: *Rosaceae*

Parts used: Leaves and roots.

Distribution

Most of the northern hemisphere including, from Iceland south and east to Iran, the Himalayas, China and Japan.

Habitat

Ditches and moist calcareous soils, it also likes sandy, gravelly soils. A common weed of cultivation. Very commonly seen by the side of roads and footpaths.

How to identify Silverweed

Silverweed is a low-growing herbaceous plant with creeping red stolons that can be up to 80 cm long. The flexible stems run along the ground, and when they contact disturbed soil they root at nodes.

The leaves are 10–20 cm long, evenly pinnate into in crenate leaflets 2–5 cm long and 1–2 cm broad, covered with silky white hairs, particularly on the underside.

The flowers are produced singly on 5–15 cm long stems, 1.5-2.5 cm diameter with five (rarely up to seven) yellow petals. The flowers grow singly from the leaf axils.

The fruit is a cluster of dry achenes.

Food

The roots can be eaten raw or cooked. It can also be dried and ground into a powder then used in soups etc or mixed with cereals. A nice taste, crisp and nutty with a somewhat starchy, parsnip-like flavour. The roots are rather thin, though perhaps their size cold be improved in cultivation.

Young shoots can be eaten raw (if you can find them!)

A tea can be made from the young leaves.

Medicine

Contemporary medical herbalists believe that silverweed's main medicinal value lies in its astringency. It is less astringent than the related Potentilla erecta, but it has a gentler action within the gastro-intestinal tract.

Known hazards

None known.

Harvesting

The roots are harvested in late summer or autumn and dried for later use. The leaves can be harvested in early summer and dried for later use.

Potential lookalikes

Cinquefoil (*Potentilla repens*) maybe? But Cinquefoil leaves are palmate.

Mythology and symbolism

The pre-Linnaean name "anserina" means "of the goose" (Anser), either because the plant was used to feed them or because the leaves reminded of the bird's footmarks. In Sweden, the flower is called gåsört (goose-wort).

A rich folklore has developed around Silverweed. The plant bears the common name of richette in French, being rich through both silver and gold.

There is a legend that the Christ child grew up and walked the roads of Palestine; and the yellow flowering plant of the dusty wayside with silvery fern-like leaves that lay flat on the ground has been called the Footsteps of Our Lord.

Potentille Ansérine. Potentilla Anserina L.

Yarrow (*Achillea millefolium*)

As children we were often told that the worse a medicine tastes, the better it is; By that reasoning alone, Yarrow flower tea must be the best medicine ever!

Key information

Common names: Arrowroot, bloodwort, death flower, eerie, field hops, gearwe, hundred leaved grass, knights milefoil, knyghten, milefolium, milfoil, millefoil, noble yarrow, nosebleed, sanguinary, seven year's love, soldier, staunchweed, thousand seal, woundwort, yarroway, yerw.

Botanical name: *Achillea millefolium*

Family: *Asteraceae*

Parts used: Flowers and leaves.

Distribution

Yarrow grows practically everywhere apart from Antarctica.

Habitat

It likes dry soils, meadows and clearings, often found along path-sides. Can grow up to 3 feet tall. Also seen frequently along canal banks.

How to identify Yarrow

It has distinctive feathery leaves, and can remain hidden amongst long grass until you look closely. The leaves are alternate. The name 'millefollium' referring to its many leaves (i.e. "thousand leaves"). It flowers from early summer to early autumn and has a composite flower head with 5 ray flowers and 10-30 disc flowers.

The leaves are evenly distributed along the stem, with the leaves near the middle and bottom of the stem being the largest. The leaves have varying degrees of hairiness. The leaves are 5–20 cm long, bipinnate or tripinnate, almost feathery, and arranged spirally on the stems. The leaves grow on the upper part of the stem, and more or less clasping.

The flowers have 4 to 9 phyllaries and contains ray and disk flowers which are white to pink. The generally 3 to 8 ray flowers are ovate to round. Disk flowers range from 15 to 40. The inflorescence is produced in a flat-topped capitulum cluster and the inflorescences are visited by many insects, featuring a generalized pollination system.

The small achene-like fruits are called cypsela.

Food

The leaves can be eaten raw or cooked. A slightly bitter flavour, they make an acceptable addition to mixed salads and are best used when young. They have a herby flavour, somewhere between parsley, dill and tarragon.

The leaves are also used as a hop-substitute for flavouring and as a preservative for beer. Alongside Mugwort as one of my favourite foraged, home-brewed beer flavours.

An aromatic tea can be made from the flowers and leaves, but can be awfully bitter.

Yarrow leaves

MEDICINE

Yarrow has a very good reputation and is widely employed and respected in herbal medicine, administered both internally and externally.

It is used in the treatment of a very wide range of disorders but is particularly valuable for treating wounds, stopping the flow of blood, treating colds, fevers, kidney diseases, menstrual pain etc.

The whole plant is used, both fresh and dried, and is best harvested when in flower.

The herb combines well with *Sambucus nigra* flowers (Elder) and *Mentha x piperita vulgaris* (Peppermint) for treating colds and influenza.

KNOWN HAZARDS

Yarrow has not been proved safe for use in pregnancy and lactation so caution is advised. Some people who are sensitive to the Asteraceae family may have a mild allergic reaction.

In rare cases, yarrow can cause severe allergic skin rashes; prolonged use can increase the skin's photosensitivity. This can be triggered initially when wet skin comes into contact with cut grass and yarrow together.

HARVESTING

The leaves seem to be available most of the year around, tender leaves appearing in early spring.

It flowers from June to August and the seeds are usually available from July to September.

POTENTIAL LOOKALIKES

I have heard it said that you could confuse Yarrow with Wild Carrot, or Hemlock. However, I find that hard to believe. Learn to recognise the characteristics and you'll be fine. For one thing, *Daucus corota* (Wild Carrot) does have vaguely similar leaves, but smells of carrot when crushed, and is edible anyway, and for another *Conium maculatum* (Hemlock) absolutely stinks and you'd be daft to put anything that smells like that in your mouth!

MYTHOLOGY AND SYMBOLISM

In the Hebrides a leaf held against the eyes was believed to give second sight.

In China, the stalks are dried and used as a randomising agent in I Ching divination.

In Greek folklore, Homer tells of the centaur Chiron, who conveyed herbal secrets to his human pupils, and taught Achilles to use yarrow on the battle grounds of Troy. This herb is named after the great Greek hero named Achilles who fought in the battle of Troy.

Achilles was the son of the goddess Thetis and the mortal Peleus, and was born a mortal. In an attempt to make her son immortal, Thetis dipped him into the River Styx. The only body part that remained mortal and vulnerable was his heel as his mother had held Achilles by one heel. Achilles grew up to be a famous hero and in the Battle of Troy Achilles used the herb Yarrow to heal his wounded soldiers. Achilles eventually was struck by an arrow on the only vulnerable spot on his body; his heel and he died.

In Egtved, Denmark they found a grave dating back to the Bronze Age. In the grave they found the remains of a woman about 20 years old. Buried along with the woman they discovered some jewellery and a yarrow plant. Yarrow followed the woman to protect her from evil spirits on her journey to the next world.

In many parts of Europe yarrow was believed to protect against all evil.

In Wales the opposite was claimed. There it was told that bringing yarrow into the home was extremely unlucky. In some areas of Wales it was even called "the death flower".

In Ireland yarrow was considered auspicious. Many used to hang yarrow around their house on midsummer night's eve to protect the household from disease the coming year.

In Scotland it was also a lucky plant. In old superstition they too claimed yarrow protected against malicious forces and used it as an amulet.

WILD STRAWBERRIES (*FRAGARIA VESCA*)

This was the forerunner to the cultivated strawberries that we grow in the UK and import from the continent. Each of the tiny fruit of the wild strawberry may seem not worth the effort, but each fruit really packs a punch of intense strawberry flavour; much more than any cultivated, imported strawberry in my opinion.

KEY INFORMATION

Common names: California strawberry, woodland strawberry, Alpine strawberry, Carpathian strawberry or European strawberry.

Botanical name: *Fragaria vesca*

Family: *Roseacea*

Parts used: Fruit, and leaves.

Distribution

Fragaria vesca grows primarily across the temperate zone of the northern hemisphere, and is introduced in sporadic places across the southern hemisphere.

Habitat

It's typical habitat is along paths and roadsides, embankments, hillsides, meadows, young woodlands, sparse forest, woodland edges, and clearings. Often plants can be found where they do not get sufficient light to form fruit. It is tolerant of a variety of moisture levels (except very wet or dry conditions).

How to identify wild strawberries

Wild strawberry is a fast growing and spreading deciduous, low growing shrub, spreading quickly to overtake wasteland, scrub and untended gardens.

Five to eleven soft, hairy white flowers are borne on a green, soft fresh-hairy 3–15 centimetres stalk that usually lifts them above the leaves.

The light-green leaves are trifoliate (in threes) with toothed margins.

The plant spreads mostly by means of runners (stolons), but the seeds are viable and can establish new populations.

Ripe wild strawberry fruit

FOOD

The fruit can be eaten raw and have an amazing intense strawberry flavour. It is aromatic, sweet and succulent and can be dried for future use.

The leaves can be used dried or fresh to make a lovely herbal tea.

MEDICINE

The leaves are astringent and have been used to treat dysentery in the past.

KNOWN HAZARDS

None known.

Harvesting

It is in flower from April to May, and the fruits ripen from June to July.

Potential lookalikes

There are different varieties of wild strawberries. All are edible, but some taste better than others.

Wild Rose Petals (*Rosa canina*)

Roses have been cultivated way back into history, so most folklore relates to those, but wild roses have been around a lot longer and can be found just about anywhere in the UK.

Key information

Common names: Dog rose, wild rose.

Botanical name: *Rosa canina*

Family: *Rosaceae*

Parts used: Flower, fruit and leaves.

Distribution

Native to Europe, northwest Africa, and Asia. Introduced in Australia and New Zealand.

Habitat

Commonly found in hedges, scrub, woods, roadsides, riverbanks, and gardens.

How to identify wild roses

Dog rose or wild rose is a fast growing deciduous shrub normally ranging in height between one and five metres on its own, but sometimes you'll see it climb much higher through taller trees. Its stems are covered with small, sharp, hooked prickles, which aid it in climbing, but do not aid us in picking! The leaves can have a sweet, rose fragrance, when bruised.

Wild roses, being wild can be highly variable. You can quite often find escaped garden varieties and of course they will readily cross-pollinate and hybridise. It's not uncommon to find white, pink, and red flowers growing close together.

The leaves are bright green, pinnate with five or seven leaflets; That is two or three opposite pairs and a terminal leaflet. The leaflets have serrated edges.

The flowers are around four to six cm in diameter, with five petals. The petals are usually pale pink but can vary from deep pink to white. The five sepals are quite unusual in that two have hairs on each side, one has hairs on one side, and the two remaining have no hairs.

The pollinated flowers mature into an oval red, hard fruit up to two cm long, called a rose hip; the dried sepals usually remain attached for a while. After a frost, the hip will darken and go soft. Inside the fruit are many seeds and irritating hairs, as well as a very tasty flesh.

Dog roses

FOOD

The dried leaves have been used as a tea substitute.

The petals can be eaten raw or included in recipes. The base of the petals can be bitter, although are a lot of effort to remove and a little bitterness is good for you. The petals can be used to make a wild Turkish delight, to flavour Elderflower champagne and to make a rose petal jam. The flowers can also be made into a syrup, candied, or preserved in vinegar, honey, or brandy.

MEDICINE

The fruit is used widely for medicinal purposes, but there are no known medicinal uses for the petals. They could be used as a flavouring to make an unpleasant tasting remedy more palatable.

KNOWN HAZARDS

None known for the petals. The whole plant has thorns which you need to be wary of.

Harvesting

The flowers have a short harvesting period, usually around June to July.

Potential Lookalikes

There are other similar rose species found in the wild in the UK, such as *Rosa rubiginosa*, *Rosa agrestis* and *Rosa acicularis*, but they are all safe to eat and have the same properties. You may also find escaped cultivated roses too. Japanese rose, *Rosa rugosa*, is quite commonly found and has big, fat hips. As with all foraging, remember not to forage plants that may have been treated with chemicals such as insect repellents.

Wild rose leaves

MYTHOLOGY AND SYMBOLISM

Whilst most folklore regarding roses refers to cultivated roses, there are a few specific to wild roses.

In Cheshire and Lancashire, it is believed that if you have an idea whilst sitting next to a dog rose, the idea will fail.

"Must not shear the sheep of its wool, Before the Dog-rose is at the full".

A late rose in the autumn was said to signify that there will be a plague, and in France some believe that smelling a dog rose will cause madness.

An old rhyme called "The Five Brethren of the Rose"[8], gives information on how to identify a dog-rose:

On a summer's day, in sultry weather

Five Brethren were born together

Two had beards and two had none

And the other had but half a one.

Rosa canina

ELDERBERRY (*SAMBUCUS NIGRA*)

According to tradition, if you want to take from the Elder tree you must ask the tree's permission. If the tree makes any sound at all, the answer is no; To take from the tree without permission means a curse and certain bad luck until you make amends...

KEY INFORMATION

Common names: Elder, elderberry, European black elderberry, European elder, European elderberry.

Botanical name: *Sambucus nigra*

Family: *Adoxaceae*

Parts used: flowers, and fruit.

Distribution

It is widespread in many temperate and sub-tropical regions of the world, and is native to the UK.

Habitat

Elder will grow in both wet and dry fertile soils, but in very wet soil the growth and fruiting can be heavily stunted. Primarily in sunny locations in woodland, scrub, hedgerows and wasteland. It often grows near rabbit warrens and badger setts where the seeds are distributed by animal droppings.

How to identify Elder

Elder is usually found as a shrub or small tree (usually up to 6 meters, but has been recorded up to 10 meters) and can live for 60 years. It is commonly characterised by its short trunk.

Like many other small trees it can grow as an upright tree or a straggly bush depending on the conditions and how it is cut back.

The bark is grey-brown, corky, deeply furrowed bark, although younger specimens have smooth grey bark.

The green unpleasant smelling twigs are hollow or have a white pith (spongy tissue) inside. New stems sometimes grow directly upwards when a branch has been cut or broken.

Buds have a ragged appearance often with leaves showing through the bud scales.

The leaves are pinnate with two to three opposite pairs (rarely four pairs) and a terminal leaflet. The leaflets are oval shaped and toothed and tend to be five to twelve centimetres long. The leaves can make an unpleasant smell when crushed.

Borne on large flat umbels, 10-30cm across, the individual flowers are tiny, creamy coloured, highly scented, and have five petals and five stamen. The smell is often compared to cat pee, but I find it quite pleasant.

Elders are hermaphrodite, meaning both the male and female reproductive parts are contained within the same flower. After pollination by insects, each flower develops into a small, purple-black, sour berry, which ripens from late-summer to autumn.

Food

The fruit can be eaten when fully cooked, or processed. The raw fruit can cause digestive upset so is best avoided if you're not used to it, though when cooked it makes delicious jams, preserves, pies and so forth. It can be used fresh or dried, the dried fruit being less bitter. The fruit is used to add flavour and colour to preserves, jams, pies, sauces, chutneys etc, it is also often used to make wine.

NOTE: The fully-ripened, raw fruit has been known to cause stomach upset in a few people – best to try a few first before gorging on them.

MEDICINE

Elder has a very long history of household use as a medicinal herb and is also much used by herbalists. The plant has been called 'the medicine chest of country people'.

The berries are packed with antioxidants, vitamin C, phenolic acids, flavonols, and anthocyanins. They are commonly used to treat colds and flu, and have been known to be very effective. Some of the constituent have be shown to fight cancer and harmful bacteria, support the immune system, and act as an antidepressant.

KNOWN HAZARDS

Every part of this plant, apart from the flowers and ripe berries, are considered toxic and should not be ingested. Some sensitivity to the ripe berries has been reported, and for those people the berries must be cooked before ingestion.

Other varieties of Sambucus have toxic berries, including the red-berried elder (for example).

HARVESTING

The flowers appear from late June and can persist into August.

POTENTIAL LOOKALIKES

Walnut (*Juglans regia*), however, elder has oppositely arranged leaves whereas walnut has alternately arranged leaves.

Identified in winter by the green unpleasant smelling twigs are hollow or have a white pith (spongy tissue) inside. Buds have a ragged appearance often with leaves showing through the bud scales.

OTHER USES

Elder wood is hard and yellow-white. Mature wood is used for whittling and carving, while smaller stems can be hollowed out to make craft items.

Elder foliage was once used to keep flies away and branches were often hung around dairies. It can also be used as an emergency insect repellent by rubbing the leaves together to get the juice out and smearing it on your skin; Be warned, it will temporarily turn your skin green and also act as a friend repellent as it smells bad.

Elder is also a great source for a variety of coloured dyes and historically it was used to make lushly patterned Harris Tweed. Blue and purple dye was obtained from the berries, yellow and green from the leaves, and grey and black dye was made from the bark.

Elder and Wildlife

The flowers provide nectar for a variety of insects and the berries are eaten by birds and mammals. Small mammals such as dormice and bank voles eat both the berries and the flowers.

Many moth caterpillars feed on elder foliage, including the white spotted pug, swallowtail, dot moth and buff ermine.

Mythology and Symbolism

There is a lot of mythology, folklore and symbolism surrounding the Elder; Here is a selection of some of the things I've read/heard:

It is thought the name elder comes the Anglo-saxon 'aeld', meaning fire, because the hollow stems were used as bellows to blow air into the centre of a fire.

It was thought that if you burned elder wood you would see the devil, but if you planted elder by your house it would keep the devil away.

Elder was also known as Judas' Tree as it was believed that Judas Iscariot hanged himself on an Elder tree.

In England it was said that if you made a baby's crib from Elder wood, the elder mother would pull the baby's legs and pinch them so they would get no rest. According to an Irish superstition, animals and children would stop growing when beaten with an elder stick.

There are stories of various types of trees which apparently cannot be struck by lightning and Elder is no exception. Apparently Elder cannot be struck by lightning because Christ's cross was made from Elder. Please don't believe this one, there are no trees that cannot be struck!

BILBERRY (*VACCINIUM MYRTILLUS*)

The UK native bilberry, is in my opinion far better than its north American relative, the blueberry. When ripe, they are tastier, juicer and probably better for you (although I might have made that up!). Of course the blueberry has the advantage in that you can just grab a punnet from a shop.

KEY INFORMATION

Common names: European blueberry, blaeberry, wimberry, whortleberry, common bilberry, blue whortleberry.

Botanical name: *Vaccinium myrtillus*

Family: *Ericaceae*

Parts used: Fruit and leaves.

DISTRIBUTION

Europe, including Britain, from Iceland south and east to Spain, Macedonia, the Caucasus and N. Asia

Habitat

It occurs in the acidic soils of heaths, moors, woods, boggy barrens, degraded meadows, open forests and parklands.

How to identify Bilberry

Vaccinium myrtillus is a small deciduous shrub that grows 10 to 40 cm tall. It has light green leaves that turn red in autumn and are simple and alternate in arrangement. Leaves are 1 to 3 cm long and ovate to lanceolate or broadly elliptic in shape.

The stem has an angled cross-section and is woody toward the base.

The flowers are up to 5mm across, reddish-pink and hang downwards from the stem. The flowers are also very tasty, but the fruit are definitely worth waiting for.

The fruit can be up to 1cm diameter, but I've never seen them quite that big. They're very dark blue and often have a pale fungal bloom on the skin making them look paler. Close inspection reveals a collar at the base of the fruit, which is the remnants of the flower. Unlike blueberries which have a white flesh, bilberries have red flesh which will stain your hands.

Bilberry flower

Food

Although small, these fruit pack quite a punch. Raw they are sweet, juicy, and sometimes a little sharp. Having very small seeds they're ideally suited for jams and jellies. They're commonly used in pies, cakes, muffins, and can also be used in sauces and syrups. The slight sharpness makes bilberries a good accompaniment for meat too.

Flowers – are lovely raw, but not as good as the fruit and quite insubstantial.

Leaves – The leaves have been used to make tea, but as far as I can tell, it's a fairly uncommon practice.

Medicine

The fruit and juice have been used in European traditional medicine for hundreds of years for various complaints. In large quantities the fruit can have a mild laxative effect; However, when dried it is astringent and can be used in the treatment of diarrhoea etc. The fruit is a rich source of anthocyanosides, which have been shown experimentally to dilate the blood vessels, this makes it a potentially valuable treatment for varicose veins, and haemorrhoids.

Known hazards

Large quantities of fruit can be mildly laxative, and there is some question as to whether it is safe to use the leaves long-term. The high tannin content could be responsible for digestive issues and is best avoided during pregnancy.

Cornucopia claims that it could interfere with blood-thinning drugs such as warfarin, so is best avoided.

Harvesting

The fruit are harvested in summer. The berries are very small, grow quite sparsely and are usually close to the ground; I strongly recommend a berry picking comb/tool.

Potential lookalikes

Maybe other wild bilberry species, but these are quite rare in the UK, and all edible anyway. In my opinion there's not really anything similar looking that grows in the same sort of places whose berries could be confused with these. If you tried really hard you might be able to confuse them with common ivy berries, or even privet, but the rest of the plant should rule those out quite quickly.

Mythology and symbolism

An interesting story from recent history is that bilberries were used by the RAF during World War 2 to improve their pilot's night vision. However, as there is no evidence to support this ability, it is most likely part of the same misinformation spread to the enemy as the story that RAF bombers ate large quantities of carrots to improve their eyesight and therefore their bombing accuracy.

BLÅBÄR, VACCINIUM MYRTILLUS L.

Penny Bun (*Boletus edulis*)

While considering these mushrooms I had to decide which common name to use, so in the end I settled for the old English name. The decision was because I know that a lot of people call the Ceps (the French name), and even more call them Porcini (the Italian name). Yes, it's true, those expensive Italian mushrooms grow wild in the UK, sometimes in huge numbers, but we have a different name for them.

Key information

Common names: Porcini, porcino, cep, king bolete.

Botanical name: *Boletus edulis*

Family: *Boletaceae*

Parts used: Cap and stipe.

Distribution

Widely distributed in the Northern Hemisphere across Europe, Asia and North America, has been introduced in the Southern hemisphere .

Habitat

Boletus edulis grows in deciduous and coniferous forests where it forms symbiotic relationships with trees, exchanging nutrients through the tree root systems.

It will often be found poking through leaf litter and grass near the base of trees, and can often be found growing in the same location as Fly Agaric mushrooms (*Amanita muscaria*).

How to identify Penny buns

The cap of this mushroom is 7–30 cm broad at maturity. Slightly sticky to touch, it is convex when young and flattens with age. It is generally reddish-brown fading to white in areas near the margin, and continues to darken as it matures. The stipe, or stem, is 8–25 cm high, and up to 7 cm thick—rather large in comparison to the cap; it is club-shaped, or bulges out in the middle. It is finely reticulate on the upper portion, but smooth or irregularly ridged on the lower part. The under surface of the cap is made of thin tubes, the site of spore production; they are 1 to 2 cm deep, and whitish in colour when young, but mature to a greenish-yellow. The spore print is olive brown. The flesh of the fruit body is white, thick and firm when young, but becomes somewhat spongy with age. When bruised or cut, it either does not change colour, or turns a very light brown or light red. Fully mature specimens can weigh about 1 kg.

Food

It is one of the most highly prized mushrooms in Europe, the excessive price of dried porcini in supermarkets shows just how prized it is.

It tastes nutty and slightly mealy, with a soft creamy texture. Both the cap and stipe are edible. It can be eaten safely raw, although as with all wild food, it is best to try a little first.

They don't keep very well, but they do keep their flavour exceptionally well when dehydrated, which is the preferred method of storing.

Pickled, or simply fried in butter are the easiest ways to use them, but they can also be added to pasta, risotto, or white sauces.

Known hazards

None known.

Harvesting

Late summer through to autumn is the best time to find these.

Potential lookalikes

The most similar poisonous mushroom is probably the devil's bolete (*Rubroboletus satanas*), which has a similar shape, but has a red stem and stains blue on bruising. It can be confused with the very bitter and unpalatable *Tylopilus felleus*, but porcini has a whitish, net-like pattern on a brownish stalk, whereas it is a dark pattern on white in the latter. If in doubt, tasting a tiny bit of flesh will yield a bitter taste.

Next Steps

So what happens now? You've read through the book, maybe you've got out and had a little practice identifying and tasting the plants and fungi, and you're wondering what the next steps for a budding forager are.

If you're looking for more seasonal plant profiles, you'll find more in the companion guides:

- Foraging for Wild Food in England – Spring edition, and
- Foraging for Wild Food in England – Autumn edition

If you're looking for inspiration for how to use your foraged bounty, we've created a companion cookbook:

- Foraging for Wild Food in England – Cookbook

And you can order them from here:
https://foundfood.com/shop/publications/

If you want to develop your knowledge even further, there is The Forager Helper, which is a web resource full of plant and fungi monographs, recipes, videos etc. which can be found at
www.foundfood.com/forager-helper

If you're starting to come across botanical terminology and you'd like some help with the scientific names, leaf and flowers structures, plant lifecycles, and other scientific words and concepts, the The Forager's Introduction to Botany is for you. You can find it here:
https://shop.foundfood.com/products/the-foragers-guide-to-botany

There's one experience which tops all of the products, and that's getting out there with a professional forager teacher. You can find my schedule here if you'd like some face-to-face learning:
https://foundfood.com/public-events/

About The Author

Gavin is passionate about understanding how plants and fungi live and work and how we can use them to our benefit without causing harm to the environment. Having had a very 'outdoors' childhood in the 1970s, Gavin spent ten years serving in the British Army where he learned about emergency food and first aid (including the beginnings of foraging and herbalism). After a second (third?) career in IT, Gavin reignited his passion for the natural world and started studying foraging in earnest. One thing led to another and before you know it he's studying herbalism and botany too, and running regular walks in and around London to introduce others to the fascinating world all around us.

Gavin formed FoundFood.com in 2012 as a personal database of his learnings, so he would always be able to look up where he had learned something from. In 2017 FoundFood.com became a blog to share some foraging related musings and experiences, them in 2023 Gavin started making his database of foraging information available to subscribers, and it has continued to grow ever since.

Now, in 2024, after many requests, Gavin has begun to release online courses and books available from www.foundfood.com